Entry Guide to Software Testing

A Beginner's Hand Book

By

Sridhar R Mallepally

Entry Guide to Software Testing

A Beginner's Hand Book

Copyright © 2010 by Parishta Inc.

21 E Middle Tpke., Manchester, CT 06042

International Standard Book Number: *978-0-9791479-1-3*
Printed in the United States of America
First Printing: August 2010

Disclaimer

This material is prepared out of vast experience of the author. Author takes no responsibility for authenticity or accuracy of the material provided.

This is not an in-depth coverage of Software testing world and author intends to give an overview of the software testing to those who intends to pursue a career in the field of testing. Author expects the readers to have minimum knowledge of software industry to understand the concepts provided in this book. QuickTest professional, LoadRunner, QualityCenter and TestDirector are the products and trademarks of Mercury Interactive/HP Software.

Acknowledgements

This book is the result of my collective experience in the field of software testing and test automation with the Mercury Interactive/HP Software at various clients across the United States and I thank everyone for giving me the opportunity to gain this experience.

I also take this opportunity to thank all my students who encouraged me to write this book with their successful entry into the testing field.

Last but not the least I am thankful to my loving wife Samatha and lovely Son Rishi, for being so co-operative with me while I was busy preparing this book.

Table of Contents

Introduction:

Software development is a complex process which involves various phases and requires various skills to put all the components together. Software Quality Assurance is a critical part of the software development process. This book is prepared to give a brief introduction to the software quality assurance aspects covering the aspects of its importance, responsibilities and opportunities in the field.

Software Testing:

Testing of the software being developed in an organization as a preventive measure to find defects in the application and to get those defects fixed before the software is released to the end users is called as software testing.

Importance of Software Testing:

Any software being developed should go through the rigorous process of testing to make sure that the software meets the requirements specified in the functional requirement document. This testing should involve both positive and negative scenarios. If the software is not tested before being released into production environment, customers/users might encounter issues with the software and the issues need to be fixed which would be a rework in the development process and results in extra time and money for the organization. Sometimes these mistakes or defects could cost the organizations millions of dollars in loss.

Who can pursue software testing as a career?

Any person with an associate degree or bachelor degree is eligible for software testing jobs. Person should have a creative approach in finding issues in the application being tested and should have a very good understanding of how the application should work. This understanding comes by going through the details specified in the functional requirement document for that application. Software tester should always have a tendency to break the application by trying different combinations in the testing environment.

Software tester should also be well versed with the latest technologies in the software industry to the level where he/she can understand how the underlying stuff works behind the application and should have good knowledge of writing SQL queries specifically, select statements. Software tester should have good understanding of the Software Development Life Cycle popularly called as SDLC.

Software Development Life Cycle (SDLC):

SDLC is a process which involves various stages in the whole software development process. This includes:

1. Initiation Phase
2. Feasibility Study
3. Documentation Phase
4. Design Phase
5. Development and Testing Phase
6. Implementation/Deployment phase
7. Post production Maintenance Phase.

Initiation Phase:

This is the first stage of SDLC where the business owner or project owner comes up with the need for the project. He/she writes the Business Requirements Document listing all the things he/she needs in that project. This document is a very broad document which just describes the needs.

Feasibility Study:

This phase involves analysis of existing resources, funds, time etc. to execute this project and based on the results of this study the team can make recommendations to the project initiator. This is a very critical phase of the SDLC where the Human Resource personnel, Finance Personnel and Software development managers need to be involved in making a decision of whether to go with the project or stall for future.

Documentation Phase:

This phase of SDLC involves preparation of documentation by the business analysts. Functional requirements document is prepared which details the entire functionality of the application to be developed including every detail of each module in the application. Use Cases are designed by breaking down the functional requirements in small details which specify what to expect at each stage of the application processing. Business analysts also design the Design Document which depicts the entire project in pieces showing each page of the application in the form of pictures.

Some organizations involve User Interface designers in this phase where they develop dummy site which acts as wireframes or prototype application for the actual application being developed. This phase acts as the guide map for the developers and testers to develop the application and test the application.

Design Phase:

In this phase, project architect prepares the conceptual design of the project and designs the data flow diagrams (DFDs) specifying how the data should flow within various modules and database is designed conceptually by the project database architect. This is a crucial phase of the SDLC on which the success of the project depends. If the architecture is poorly designed there will be a need to revisit this phase from time to time in the development process and could take more time and development rework effort on part of developers.

Development and Testing:

This phase involves the developers in developing the application using a programming language which the organization chooses and the testers test the entire application to see if the application is built according to the functional requirements document and design document.

This phase is the longest phase in the entire SDLC process and is a very crucial phase.

Implementation/Deployment phase:

This phase involves in making the application visible and available to end users. This is the last phase in the actual development phase of the software. By this phase all the infrastructure and servers should be ready and Secured Socket Layers (SSLs) applied for the pages where security is a concern.

Post Production Maintenance Phase:

After the application is deployed to production environment where the users can access the application, there is always a chance that the users find issues while using the application. These issues are logged into the organization's defect tracking system from where the development team gets to work on fixing these issues.

In the process of fixing the issues there might be a need to revisit any or all of the phases above and that is the reason why the whole process is called a cycle which is never ending. As the new features are suggested and added to the software as the business grows, there is always a need to revisit all or some of the above phases and cycle continues.

Software Development Methodologies:

In the process of software development evolution, many methodologies were proposed and followed in the industry. Few of the popular methodologies are:

Waterfall Methodology

Waterfall methodology proposes a sequence of development steps in order which helps in ensuring the adequacy of documentation and design reviews to achieve the quality, reliability, and maintainability of the developed software. This methodology puts emphasis on perfection of each stage before going to the next phase of the project. Though "waterfall methodology" is slow and cumbersome, it does have sound principles of life cycle development.

All projects can be managed better when segmented into small chunks such as phases, activities, tasks and steps and the perfection is attained at each stage. This methodology unfortunately is not suitable for the fast phased or dynamically changing software industry where the needs and technology changes every day and by the time we reach the final stage, the technology might get updated or outdated. This methodology can best suite the long term projects like defense projects. A graphical representation of waterfall methodology:

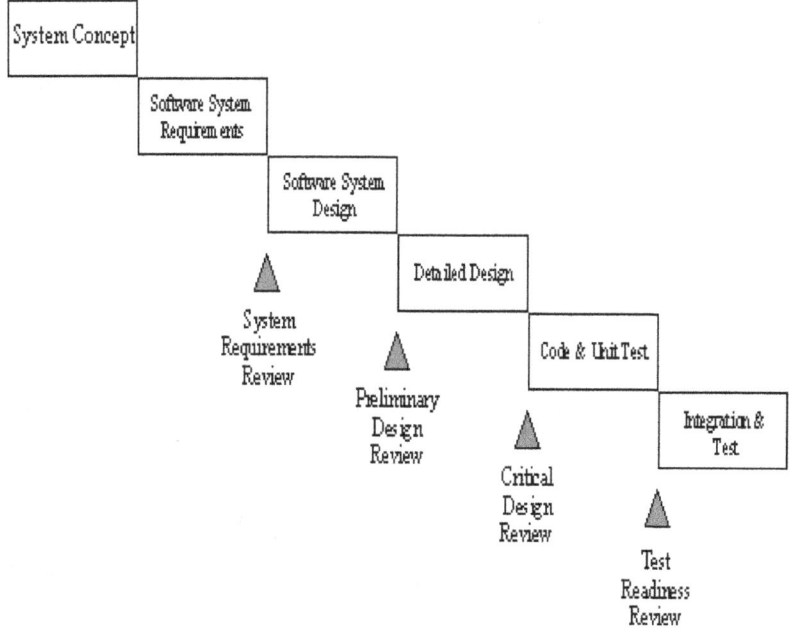

In looking at the above picture, note that this presumes that the system requirements have already been defined and scrubbed thoroughly which is, the most important step towards the success of the project.

Main Features of waterfall methodology:

- Work is done in stages/phases, and perfection is attained at each phase.
- Reviews are conducted between stages, and
- Reviews represent quality gateways and decision points for continuing.
- There is no way of going back to the previous phase.

Spiral Methodology:

In order to reduce the time of the software development process to meet the fast paced demand for the delivery of the software, spiral methodology was proposed. The spiral, aims at projects being incremental and iterative, where the team will be able to start small and benefit from enlightened trial and error along the way.

Spiral methodology involves rapid prototyping. Software design and build activities are carried out simultaneously. The spiral method should still be planned methodically, with tasks and deliverables identified for each step in the spiral.

Spiral Development Model

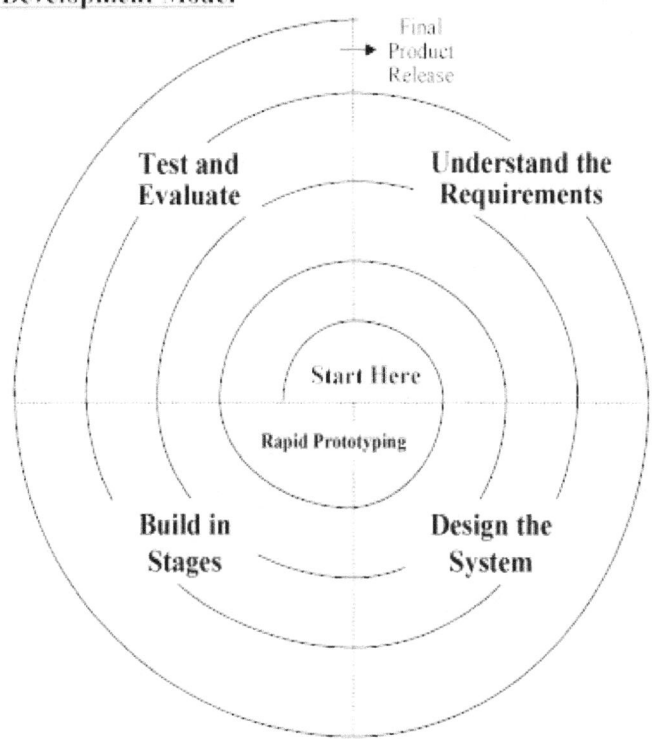

Spiral Methodology is more flexible and repetitive. It starts with a rapid prototyping of the requirements to start off the project, design the system and we can go back to the requirement changes if there is a need while designing the system. Build the system in stages and while building the system we can always go back and change the requirements or design of the

13

system if there is a need. Testers and developers should understand the requirements and there is always a way to go back and change the requirements or design of development when the system is being tested and if the team feels that there should be change in any of the above phases they can always change them.

Though this methodology is very flexible, there is a lot of chaos or confusion arising due to this flexibility and this methodology takes a long time to get the product to the perfection as the last minute changes are always allowed in this methodology.

V-Model

The V-model is a software development model which can be presumed to be the extension of the waterfall model. Instead of moving down in a linear way, the process steps are bent upwards after the coding phase, to form the typical V shape. The V-Model demonstrates the relationships between each phase of the development life cycle and its associated phase of testing.

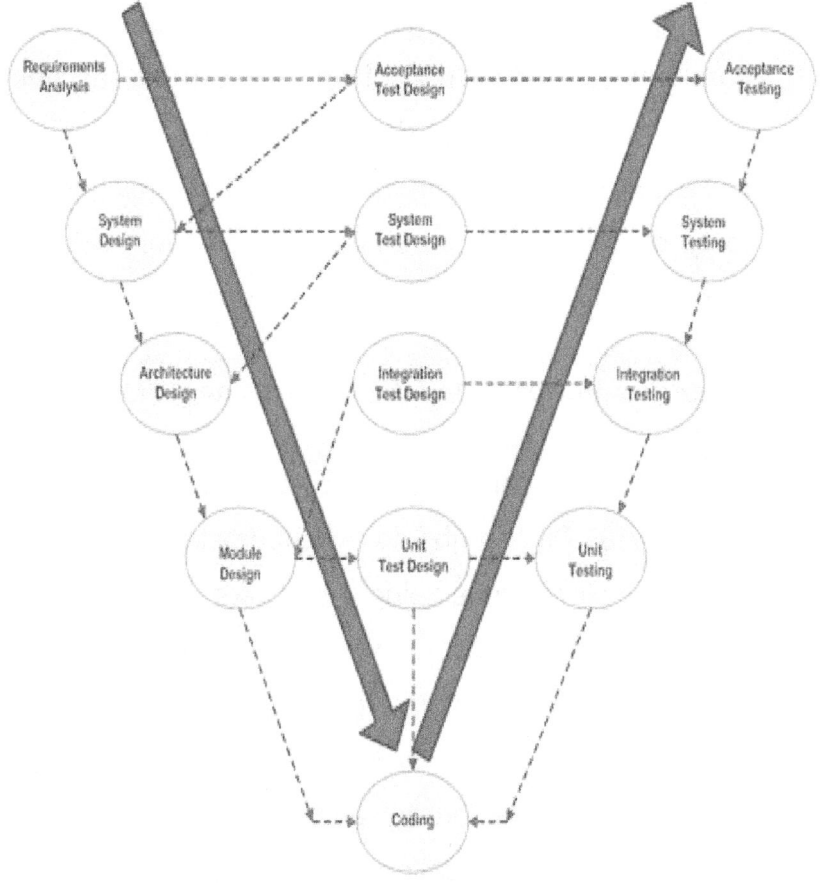

The V-model deploys a well-structured method in which each phase can be implemented by the detailed documentation of the previous phase. Testing activities like test designing start at the beginning of the project well before coding and therefore saves a huge amount of the project time.

15

V-model can be defined as more flexible and structural approach of software designing as the system is perfected and designed in stages and while in the testing process there is always a provision of going back to the appropriate development stage to fix the issues arising in the testing process.

Capability Maturity Model® Integration (CMMI):

Software Engineering Institute at Carnegie Mellon Institute in Pittsburgh established standards and guidance for developing software engineering disciplines and management. This is designed specifically for the software industry. This was known as the Capability Maturity Model (CMM), and its use has become widespread among mature software development organizations, especially for those developing large scale software in a competitive procurement environment. Government and corporate software customers have increasingly required that proposals include information about a software development organization's certified level of maturity. The CMM had recognized five steps towards organizational software maturity:

Level 1 (Initial) - Processes are *ad hoc* and occasionally chaotic. Few processes are defined, and success depends on individual effort and heroics. *(A street-person with a laptop would be at Level 1.)*

Level 2 (Repeatable) - Basic project management processes are established to track cost, schedule and functionality. A process discipline is in place to repeat earlier successes on projects with similar applications.

Level 3 (Defined) - Management and engineering processes are documented and integrated into a standard software process. Projects use an approved, tailored version of the organization's standard software process.

Level 4 (Managed) - Detailed measures of the software process and product quality are collected. Processes and products are quantitatively understood and controlled.

Level 5 (Optimizing) - Continuous process improvement is aided by quantitative feedback from the process and from piloting innovative ideas and technologies.

Around year 2000, the SEI introduced the next major evolution along this path – called Capability Maturity Model® Integration (CMMI). This builds on the previous CMM, which is now regarded as "legacy" and no longer supported.

Agile Methodology:

Agile methodology is a popular methodology being used in most of the organizations in the current days where the software needs change dynamically. Agile methods promote a disciplined project management process that encourages frequent inspection and adaptation, a leadership philosophy that encourages teamwork, self-organization and accountability, a set of engineering best practices intended to allow for rapid delivery of high-quality software, and a business approach that aligns development with customer needs and company goals.

Agile methods emphasis on breaking tasks into small increments with minimal planning, and do not directly involve long-term planning. Iterations are short time frames ("timeboxes") that typically last from one to four weeks. Each iteration involves a team working through a full software development cycle including planning, requirements analysis, design, coding, unit testing, and acceptance testing when a working product is demonstrated to stakeholders. This helps minimize overall risk, and lets the project adapt to changes quickly. Stakeholders produce documentation as required. An iteration may not add enough functionality to warrant a market release, but the goal is to have an available release (with minimal bugs) at the end of each iteration. Multiple iterations may be required to release a product or new features.

Team composition in an agile project is usually cross-functional and self-organizing without consideration for any existing corporate hierarchy or the corporate roles of team members. Team members normally take responsibility for tasks that deliver the functionality an iteration requires. They decide individually how to meet an iteration's requirements.

Agile methods emphasize face-to-face communication over written documents when the team is all in the same location. When a team works in different locations, they maintain daily contact through videoconferencing, voice, e-mail, etc.

Most agile teams work in a single open office (called bullpen), which facilitates such communication. Team size is typically small (5-9 people) to help make team communication and team collaboration easier. Larger development efforts may be delivered by multiple teams working toward a common goal or different parts of an effort. This may also require a coordination of priorities across teams.

No matter what development disciplines are required, each agile team will contain a customer representative. This person is appointed by stakeholders to act on their behalf and makes a personal commitment to being available for developers to answer mid-iteration problem-domain questions. At the end of each iteration, stakeholders and the customer representative review progress and re-evaluate priorities with a view to optimizing the return on investment and ensuring alignment with customer needs and company goals.

Most agile implementations use a routine and formal daily face-to-face communication among team members. This specifically includes the customer representative and any interested stakeholders as observers. In a brief session, team members report to each other what they did yesterday, what they intend to do today, and what their roadblocks are. This standing face-to-face communication termed as scrum meetings prevent problems from being hidden.

Agile emphasizes working software as the primary measure of progress. This, combined with the preference for face-to-face communication, produces less written documentation than other methods. The agile method encourages stakeholders to prioritize wants with other iteration outcomes based exclusively on business value perceived at the beginning of the iteration.

Specific tools and techniques such as continuous integration, automated tests, pair programming, test driven development, design patterns, domain-driven design, code refactoring and other techniques are often used to improve quality and enhance project agility.

Advantages of Agile Methodology:

- Customer satisfaction by rapid, continuous delivery of useful software
- Working software is delivered frequently (weeks rather than months)
- Working software is the principal measure of progress
- Even late changes in requirements are welcomed
- Close, daily cooperation between business people and developers
- Face-to-face conversation is the best form of communication (co-location)
- Projects are built around motivated individuals, who should be trusted
- Continuous attention to technical excellence and good design
- Simplicity
- Self-organizing teams
- Regular adaptation to changing circumstances

Importance of Software Testing in Software Development Process:

QA is one aspect which is very important in the Software Development Life Cycle. Tester will be part of the team which is responsible for the quality of application being delivered. Also, QA has broad opportunities and large scope for learning various technologies. Irrespective of the platform in which the application is being developed QA process remains more or less the same thus forming the best practices to be followed.

Common myths about QA/Testing field:

1. **Testing is the least important functionality and tester is not given much importance.**

   Testing is the most important part of the software development projects since the tester finds the defects in the applications before the application is visible to the end user. Management is realizing this importance and these days in most of the organizations testers are given the most priority and importance as they eventually act as the gate keepers of the software being pushed to production.

2. Testing is the easiest job in the software development process.

Well, testing can involve no coding on the development of the application but to be a successful tester one needs to be perfect with the entire application and needs to keep him/herself updated with the requirement changes for every release of the application. This gives the testers an edge over the developers since developers only are aware of the modules which they develop. Testers also need to prepare the detailed test cases with both positive and negative scenarios keeping in mind the entire application and intertwined functionality of the proposed changes in the application for each release. This needs a lot of skill and concentration on part tester which is not really an easy thing to achieve. Most projects require the data validation process and this requires the tester to have good skills writing the SQL queries (select statements) to extract the data from the database and compare against the expected results.

3. No formal training is needed to work as a Tester. Anyone can be a Tester.

To be a good tester one should be well aware of the Software Development principles which are followed in the industry and should also be aware of how the underlying language in which the software is being developed works so he/she can discuss the issues confidently with the developers. This definitely needs some kind of formal training and to be a good tester one should be well aware of writing the good test cases analyzing the application's functional requirements to see none of the functional requirements are being left without being tested.

4. Testing does not offer any career growth.

This is absolutely incorrect. Tester is the person who is well aware of the entire functionality of the application and in most service oriented organizations the knowledge of the application could be knowledge of the entire company's business. He/she can grow to a Business analyst position and QA manager's position and with additional certifications available in the testing field he/she can always get the desired promotions. Irrespective of the underlying technology behind the application being developed, tester can test the application with his experience and thus it offers wide range of job offers to change and grow in the career.

Difference between Quality Assurance (QA) and Quality Control (QC)

Quality Assurance (QA) is the process of defining the rules, regulations and methods followed in the organization to constantly improve the quality of the products developed within the organization. This is purely a management function.

Quality Control (QC) is the actual process of testing the products developed or being developed. The human interference is involved and using the processes defined by QA department the quality of the product is measured and certified by the Quality Control department. This is purely a people function.

QA should be involved in the process of Software Development Life Cycle (SDLC) right from the initiation of the project. This helps the QA resources in understanding the requirements well and will have enough time to plan various kinds of test cases both Positive and Negative. But in the current industry, many organizations are hiring QA resources just one to three months before the implementation of the application in production. This can result in a poor QA with respect to the scenarios to be tested.

As any of the formal processes Quality Assurance too has a life cycle to be followed. This document is an effort to enumerate the various stages in the QA Life Cycle.

QA process intends to look into the overall quality of the application. It is a systematic process, which attempts to look into, various aspects impacting the quality of the application. QA is basically a preventive approach in the process of application development to minimize the cost of development and maintenance. QA team has to be in constant interaction with the Business Analysts to know the latest changes in the requirements or additional requirements added, and with the development team to know the changes they make in the application, to report any defects found in the testing process and to recommend the fine tuning of the application or database based on the test results.

The process of QA starts with the initiation of the project request and gets into action when the requirements are gathered and documented.

QA Process depends basically on the following documents:

1. Business requirements Document (BRD)
2. System Requirements Specifications (SRS)
3. Functional Requirement Document (FRD)
4. Use cases
5. Technical Specifications.

Steps involved in a QA Process:

A. Analysis and Documentation Phase
B. Testing Phase
C. Defect Tracking Phase
D. Analysis and Documentation of the test results

A. **Analysis and Documentation:** The first step would be to analyze the requirements and document the purpose of the QA effort. This is required for the proper communication between the QA Team, Business Analysts and the Development team.

This document should specify the characteristics of the QA environment, like hardware, software and any tools used in the process of testing the application. It should also speak about the configuration of the servers, disk space, memory requirements and size of the databases.

It should specify the proposed schedule of milestones in the process of testing.

We might require more than one QA environment if we anticipate frequent releases or upgrades to the application.

A Test Plan Assessment Document has to be prepared which will be serving as the standard template for the testers in preparing the perfect standardized Test Plan document.

A Test Plan Document has to be prepared with the details of the testing effort being conducted. This document should include the following:
1.   Purpose of the testing effort
2.   Need for this testing effort.

3.   Environment used for this testing.

4.   Boundaries of the testing effort.

5.   Entry and Exit Criteria.

6.   Scope of this testing.

7.   Resources needed or involved.

8.   Definitions used if any.

9.   Time frame needed for this testing.

10.   Risk factors involved in this testing effort.

11.   Detailed Test Cases.

B. Testing Phase:

Stages in Testing/Types of Testing

White Box Testing:

Testing of the application while the code is visible to the tester so he can modify the code to fix the issue on the fly is called White Box testing. These white box testing phases are to be carried over by the development team who are expert in the coding process and who are responsible to develop the application. It involves the following stages:

1. **Unit Testing:** This is the effort carried out by the developers in which they validate that their individual units/programs are working fine.

2. **Integration Testing:** Integration testing is carried out by the developers in which they integrate their individual units and make sure their integration works fine.

3. **System Testing:** System Testing is to test the working of the entire application as a system. In this effort we need to test the application keeping in view all the interfaces and connectivity from, and, to the application, like database servers, web servers, application servers, external connections like credit card processing system (Merchant Processor) etc. This effort, is usually carried out by the development team, but yet times QA is also involved.

Black Box Testing:

Testing of application where the tester can't see the code or not authorized to modify the code underlying the application is called Black Box testing. These phases of testing are carried over by QA testers. The stages involved in this type of testing are:

4. **Confidence Testing/Build Acceptance Testing:** This is the testing carried out by QA when the application code is moved into QA Environment to see that the application is up and running and there are no configuration issues or data issues due to migration of the code from Development environment into QA Environment.

5. **Functional Testing:** This testing is carried by the QA to test that the application is performing all the intended functions perfectly without any errors. In this QA will test the application using various scenarios. Both positive testing and negative testing will be performed.

   Positive testing will involve passing the correct values as specified in the Functional Requirements and make sure that the application is processing them properly.

   Negative testing will involve passing the values which are not supposed to be returning the correct results and look for the proper error messages displayed by the application.

6. **Regression Testing:** Regression Testing is carried out after each release along with the Functional testing of the new functionality. The purpose of this testing is to see that nothing is broken with the existing code while the developers are developing new functionality or fixing the defects from the earlier functional testing. This is usually carried out by the automation tools like QuickTest Professional® in which the scripts are run to check that nothing is being broken. This needs a test bed to be created in QuickTest Professional® with all the scripts which test the major functionality of the application.

7. **Load/ Performance/ Stress testing:**
Load/performance testing is carried by QA to make sure that the application can handle the anticipated traffic and load. This is carried out by using Load Testing tools like LoadRunner. In this test we will monitor the performance of

the Web server, database server, application server, CPU usage of the server, memory usage of the server. When the Load test is carried for a prolonged time like say for 8 hours continuously to see that the application can sustain high loads of work for any number of hours, it is called **Stress** Testing. Load/Stress testing is carried out only after the Functionality of the application is working fine, in other words when Functional Testing is certified by QA.

8. **User Acceptance/Acceptance Testing:** This is usually, carried out by the user groups or customers. This is to make sure that the actual customer/end user is satisfied with the overall look, feel and functionality of the application.

9. **Smoke Testing:** This is the post-production testing to make sure that nothing is broken while migrating the application code from the QA environment into the production environment.

C. Defect Tracking:

This is the crucial part of the QA testing effort. The defects found in every kind of testing have to be logged into defect tracking tool or they should be properly documented and communicated to the development team. Based on the priority and severity of the defect, developers fix the defects and change the status of the defect to Fixed and QA team will have to re-test these defects and either Close the defect if QA is satisfied with the bug fix or re-open the defect. If the development is rejecting the defect they should give the proper reason for that and if the QA is not satisfied with the explanation the problem should be escalated to the QA Manager and thereby to the Project Manager depending on the severity of the defect.

Classifying the severity and priority of the defect

If a defect is a show stopper and we can't continue our testing without that being fixed it needs to be classified as Severity Level 1 and High Priority, if it is a missing functionality but if there is a work around for that and it is not stopping the tester from testing the rest of the application it should be classified as Severity Level 2. If it is a cosmetic defect like some typing errors it should be classified as Low Priority and Low severity. Each organization has its own definitions for the severity level of the defects and tester should follow them.

Conflict with the developer on a defect

At times there will be conflict with the developer on the defects the testers find. In this situation tester should try to convince the developer by recreating the defect and if the developer still disagrees with the tester, he needs to show proper reasons and clarify it with the Business Analysts and if the BA also sees this as a defect this should be escalated this to the QA Manager and ultimately to the Project Manager to keep them in loop.

D. Analysis and Documentation of the test results:

After a testing effort is finished successfully QA Team has to analyze the test results and document the results giving every detail, which they think is important and necessary. This gives an opportunity for the QA team to provide the recommendations to the application development team, database administrators, server administrators and to the infrastructure team in the QA review meetings or application team meetings.

Responsibilities of a QA Tester

QA Tester will need to understand the project documentation such as Functional Requirements Document, System Requirements Document and Use Case Documents.

QA Tester will prepare the test plan and include the test cases classifying them according to the functionality of the application say for example: Login is one functionality and it should include only the test cases pertaining to that only and this could be created as a heading Customer_Login, etc.

QA Tester should analyze the application and decide which parts can be automated and which parts are to be tested manually. He/She needs to develop the automation test scripts for those parts which can be automated. Also he/she should judge whether it is worth automating those parts since some functionalities might take too much of time to write script using automation tools and that actually might take a few minutes of time to test manually.

QA Tester should always think of the various possibilities of breaking the application and for that purpose he/she needs to think of all kinds of negative scenarios for testing.

QA Tester needs a good understanding and command on SQL as he/she is supposed to test the database validations also. He/She should also be ready to learn and adapt to any technology as different clients might ask testers to use a different tool.

QA tester is responsible for carrying the end to end testing of the application in all the perspectives both manually and using automation tools.

Documents to be prepared by the tester:

QA tester might need to prepare some or all of these documents depending on the situation.

- Test Plan (Word or Excel)
- Test Cases
- Test Strategy document
- Test Execution Metrics (Excel) weekly reports
- Defect Metrics (Excel)
    1. Number of defects in the system
    2. Number of defects opened this week
    3. Number of defects fixed
    4. Number of defects retested
    5. Number of defects closed
    6. Number of defects Reopened
- Automation Status Report
    1. Total Number of test cases
    2. Number of test cases automated
    3. Number of test cases to be automated next week
    4. Number of test case in the maintenance mode
- Templates (Test Case template)

Responsibilities of a QA Lead

The QA Lead will be an integral part of the leadership team.

QA Lead will be responsible for coordinating the overall testing efforts for multiple concurrent projects.

QA Lead will be expected to actively participate in project team meetings to gain an in-depth understanding of the application to be developed and voice QA needs.

QA Lead will be expected to apply appropriate Quality Assurance processes and procedures to the assigned projects. This will include developing a test strategy, identifying the QA tasks for the project plan, overseeing the construction of test cases, and helping to estimate testing time frames and resources needed for a project.

QA Lead will need to identify the environments for the QA Testing, Load Testing, User Acceptance Testing and also identify the servers for each environment and make sure they are available for his projects.

QA Lead will also gather the test data from the customers if needed for the testing purposes.

QA Lead will need to interpret requirements and use case documents and be able to coordinate and participate in the creation and execution of test cases.

QA Lead will document defects and collaborate with development and project managers to see defects through to resolution. In addition, the QA Lead will document test results and communicate the status of testing to the project team and management.

QA Lead should understand and make recommendations regarding the use of automated testing tools for a particular project.

QA Lead will also work closely with the automation team to ensure that a robust regression test bed is created. While performing the above tasks, this person will also have the opportunity to review the current Quality Assurance processes, procedures, and templates in place and provide feedback for future improvements.

QA Lead will be responsible to provide the reports of test execution before the project is being implemented and make recommendations to improving the quality of the application based on the test results.

Interaction of QA tester with other team members:

QA testing is an integral part of the software development process and in this process tester needs to interact with the team members. As a QA resource QA team needs to interact with the Business Analysts to understand the business rules and logic and they can provide QA with the requirement documents. QA tester needs to make a list of the names of the persons who deal with different aspects of the project like Business Analysts, Developers, Networking team, Database Administrators, System Administrators, Project Leader and Project Manager. Tester might need to interact with any of the above as the situation demands.

Typical Software Development and Testing Environment:

Though organizations have different development structures depending on the software they use and methodology they use, they more or less follow a common practice as outlined below.

Developers will be writing the code on their desktops which are called as local hosts. Once the coding is done and unit testing is finished the code is checked into the development server which is a common property of the development team. Checked in code from all the developers is built into an application through a nightly job and some organizations might do an on-demand daily builds on the development server. The application on this server is in a very primitive and volatile stage and can't be used to test the entire functionality of the application. When a build request is made by the QA team, development lead

44

runs a Code generation (CodeGen) process which integrates the database schema changes with the code changes in the application. Then the application code will be deployed to the Build server and at this stage QA can be involved in performing the build acceptance testing or confidence testing. Once that is done development lead will install the application on the QA Test server and perform the confidence testing again to see they don't have any issues with the server configurations and if found satisfactory will continue the Functional Testing and Regression Testing. If the application fails the confidence tests the code will be rolled back to the previous version and development team needs to look at the cause of the problem. Once the functional and regression testing phases are QA certified, the application will be installed on the Load Testing environment where the Load Test is carried out using an automation tool like LoadRunner. If the application is found stable enough to be moved into the Acceptance Testing it will be installed in User Acceptance Testing environment where the Users will test and certify the product before going to the production.

Typically a week before the testing begins, Release manager (in some cases it is business analyst) should co-ordinate with all the developers and find out the changes going into that release and publish or email the change log to the entire team so everyone is aware of what is going into the release. Each change made by the developers is associated with the change set which has a unique id generated by the development tool. If the change set is the result of a defect fix entered in the defect tracking system, the defect Id should be specified in the change log.

In most organizations they maintain two types of defect tracking systems. There will be a corporate wide defect tracking system which is used by all employees of the organization to log in the defects or problems they face. These could be either the issues using the application, any hardware related issues or requests for the password resets, new system installation for a new employee etc. Only production issues should be logged into this defect tracking system. Some of the popular corporate-wide defect tracking systems are Remedy, Gemini, Scarab etc. There is another kind of defect tracking system which is used by the IT staff to track the IT related (application related in specific). When a production application related issue is entered through the corporate wide defect tracking system, the person who is in-charge of maintaining that system will create an entry in the defect tracking system used by the IT staff so the developers can work on fixing these issues. In such case the defect ID from Corporate defect tracking system is associated to the IT defect tracking system. Some popular defect tracking systems used by IT staff are QualityCenter from HP Software, Team Foundation Suite (TFS) from Microsoft, Rational ClearQuest from IBM etc.

Sample Test Case:

Browser: Internet Explorer Version: 7.0	URL used: http://onsitetraining.net Environment: QA		User ID: Password:
Test Objective:	To test the login page for functionality and usability.		
Assumptions & Pre-work:			
Requirements Tested:	Login requirements by performing both positive and negative scenarios.	Date-Time Started	
Conditions Tested:	This test case covers both positive and negative scenarios.	Date-Time Ended	

Ste p #	Description/Inp uts	Expected Result	Differences – Defect# – Comments	P/F
1	Invoke browser by clicking on Internet Explorer icon	The Home page displays		
2	Enter the URL and press "enter"	Onsitetraining.net website login page should open.		
3	User Verifies	• The wording Onsitetraining should be displayed on the left hand bottom portion of the login area and the version number should be displayed at the right hand bottom corner of the login area. • The fields UserName and Password should be displayed as edits and are editable. • A link should be displayed which says : "New Users should click here to register"		
Negative Scenarios:				
4	Press SignIn button without entering either username or password	Red stars should appear on the right hand corner of each edit box which indicate that these are mandatory. Proper error message should be displayed asking to enter the username and password.	No message is being displayed right now. Defect ID # 931 in TFS opened to address this issue.	
5	Enter username in the Username field and click on Sign in button.	Red Star beside the Username field should disappear.		
6	Enter correct username and wrong password	Error message "Your login attempt was not successful. Please try again." Should be displayed		

Step #	Description/Inputs	Expected Result	Differences – Defect# – Comments	P/F
	and click Sign in.	below the login fields.		
7	Leave the username blank and type in the correct password and click Sign In.	Error message "Your login attempt was not successful. Please try again." Should be displayed below the login fields. Star should be displayed by the side of username field.		
8	Leave the password blank and type in the correct username and click Sign In.	Error message "Your login attempt was not successful. Please try again." Should be displayed below the login fields. Star should be displayed by the side of username field.		
Positive Scenarios:				
9	Enter the valid username and password and click Sign In button.	User should be successfully logged into the application.		
10	Click on Logoff link on top of the application	Should be logged out of application.		
11	Enter valid username in the Username field login screen.	Password should not be prefilled.		
12	Click on the link "New Users should click here to register"	User Registration page should be displayed.		

In the above sample test case:

Top header is for documentation or informational purposes and also for providing any pre-required information to the tester executing the test case.

49

This sample Test case is broken down into sections positive and negative scenarios for the clarity purposes.

Date-Time started and Date-Time ended are fields which should be filled in while execution of the test case to see how long it took to execute the test case.

"Differences-Defect#-Comments" column is optional and provides the testing who is executing the test case with extra information needed while executing the test case. If there is already a defect in the test case, speficying that defect ID on the test case helps to avoid duplication of the defects in the defect tracking system.

"P/F" section is also optional and is used by the tester executing the test case to mention if the test step has passed or failed.

Index

52

Also by Sridhar R Mallepally

THIS BOOK PRESENTS QUICKTEST PROFESSIONAL 10 IN EASY TO UNDERSTAND WORDS WITH REAL-TIME EXAMPLES AND ILLUSTR ILLUSTRATIONS. THIS GUIDE WALKS YOU THROUGH THE STEP BY STEP PROCESS OF SETTING UP YOUR AUTOMATION SCRIPTS TO TEST ANY KIND OF APPLICATION. ALSO, PROVIDED ARE THE MOST COMMONLY USED FUNCTIONS AND BEST PRACTICES FOLLOWED IN THE INDUSTRY. ALL CONCEPTS ARE EXPLAINED IN PLAIN WORDS FOR EASY UNDERSTANDING AND THE GUIDE ALSO HAS THE MOST COMMONLY ASKED INTERVIEW QUESTIONS AND ANSWERS TO THEM.

QUICKTEST PROFESSIONAL INTERVIEW QUESTIONS AND GUIDELINES - REFERENCE GUIDE
Publisher: Parishta Inc.
$16:00 USA

Parishta

About the Publisher:

Parishta Inc. is a publisher of educational and reference books in the field of Software Technology.

Contact Information:
Parishta Inc.
21 E Middle Tpke.
Manchester, CT – 06042
United States of America.
Phone: 860-432-9956
Fax: 888-490-2581
eMail: support@parishta.com
Website: http://www.Parishta.com

Made in the USA
Monee, IL
07 July 2026

56552276R00036